PRAYERS
for every occasion

PRAYERS
for every occasion

Compiled by
DON SANFORD

ZONDERVAN PUBLISHING HOUSE
OF THE ZONDERVAN CORPORATION
GRAND RAPIDS, MICHIGAN 49506

PRAYERS FOR EVERY OCCASION
Copyright 1957 by Zondervan Publishing House
Grand Rapids, Michigan

ISBN 0-310-32582-X

A Word to You . . .

Prayer is infinitely more than simply the use of words in addressing the Heavenly Father. Prayer is really an attitude of heart.

The prayers gathered in this book are not compiled for recitation by rote or to be read without attention to meaning. They *are* intended for God's people as a guide to more meaningful communion with God. If all they do is to stimulate a spirit of closeness with and devotion to God, these prayers will have accomplished their purpose. Or, if they serve as a model to one new Christian who earnestly seeks to grow spiritually, they will have proved their worth.

DON SANFORD

Printed in the United States of America

THIS BOOK WILL HELP YOU . . .

Praying through the Day
Morning Prayers 5
Grace Before Meals 7
Thanks After Meals 13
Evening and Bedtime Prayers 17
Bedtime Prayers for Children 18

Praying in Public
Prayers for Repentance and Confession 19
Prayers for Guidance 23
Prayers for One's Country 26
Prayers for the Afflicted and Shut-ins,
the Poor and Needy 29
Prayers for the Armed Forces 37
Prayers of Devotion...................................... 38
A Prayer for a Newborn Child 47
Prayers for Bereaved Families 48
Prayers for Forgiveness 50
Prayers of Worship and Thanksgiving 54

Praying on Special Days
Christmas 60
New Year's Day 64

Palm Sunday	67
Good Friday	68
Easter	69
Mother's Day	74
Memorial Day	75
Fourth of July	77
Labor Day	78
Thanksgiving	79

PRAYING ON SPECIAL OCCASIONS

For Youth	80
For a Sick Child	81
For Peace	82
For Love	85
For a Newly Married Couple	86

PRAYING AS A SUNDAY SCHOOL TEACHER 87-91

PRAYING AS A YOUTH LEADER 92-95

PRAYING AS A PASTOR

Invocations	96
Worship and Dedication	104

SENTENCE PRAYERS 116-121

PRAYERS
for every occasion

PRAYING THROUGH THE DAY

Morning Prayers

O God, help us that we may rise up and follow Thee with joyful and willing hearts. Make us patient to do Thy will this day. Come to our waiting souls as swift as the light of the morning. Give us courage and hope to make this new day a day of victory. In our Saviour's Name. Amen.

Our Precious Lord, Thou hast brought us safely through the night into this glorious new day. Waken our minds and stimulate our hesitating wills. Give us courage and patience in whatever trial may come to us. May we use to the glory of Thy Name the precious hours of today. The night cometh soon. At the close of life's day may we receive Thy welcome into the Father's House: "Well done, good and faithful servant." In Jesus' Name we pray. Amen.

PRAYING THROUGH THE DAY

Morning Prayers

Most Gracious Lord, we come to Thee with thankful hearts for the night of rest Thou hast given us. Now Thou hast brought to us this glorious new day. May the Sun of righteousness with healing in His wings be our companion this day. We do not know what the day may bring forth, but we are content to take one step at a time if Thou wilt lead us. Give us, O Lord, Thy wisdom and grace. Amen.

O most loving Saviour, in the light of this new day may the sunshine of Thy presence shine upon our souls. Dispel the darkness from our minds and wills, teach us how we should walk and what we should do. We thank Thee for the opportunity of duties and responsibilities before us. Give us willing hearts that we may patiently and faithfully toil this blessed day so that, at its close, we can say truly, this was one more day's work for Thee. In Thy Name. Amen.

**PRAYING THROUGH
THE DAY**

MORNING PRAYERS

Our Heavenly Father, we thank Thee for the refreshing sleep Thou hast given us. Now, Thou hast brought us from the night to this glorious new day. Inspire us, O Father, with new hope, new courage, to take up the problems that await our solution. Thou, who knowest all things, control our minds and cheer our hearts. May we have Thy Grace as we greet this day with expectant minds and obedient wills. Merciful Father, lead us hour to hour, in all the cares and duties which await us. In Thy Name. Amen.

GRACE BEFORE MEALS

For the continuance of Thy loving kindness unto us, we give Thee all thanks, O Lord. Fulfill all our needs and sustain us, for Jesus' sake. Amen.

Do Thou bless our meal today, and may Thy Presence fill us with gratitude for all these abundant blessings. Amen.

PRAYING THROUGH THE DAY

GRACE BEFORE MEALS

Thou hast saved and preserved us, O Lord, and may we by our lives never bring reproach upon the Name of Jesus, but ever learn to live for Thee, and to Thy honor. Amen.

Lord, wilt Thou never cease Thy kindly care over us, and may we also continue unceasingly to bless Thee for all Thy past and present blessings. In Jesus' Name. Amen.

Give us grace to be grateful for the blessings which Thou hast so bountifully spread before us today. In Thine own Name. Amen.

O Thou, who satisfieth our mouths with good things, we praise Thee for Thy gracious providence, and invoke Thy blessing as we partake. Amen.

Grace Before Meals

We give Thee thanks for life and all its blessings. Give Thou this food to nourish our bodies, and Thy Word of Truth to sustain our souls. Amen.

Keep us ever humble, Lord, that we may be the ready recipients of Thy goodness. Deliver us from pride and wickedness, and supply our wants. In Thy Name. Amen.

O Lord, we thank Thee for life and the joy of living, for health and strength, and for these blessings fresh from Thy hand of love. Through Jesus Christ, our Lord. Amen.

All things come of Thee, O Lord, and for these and all Thy blessings we give hearty thanks, in the Name of Christ our Redeemer. Amen.

Bless, O Lord, this food to our use, and us in Thy service, through Jesus Christ our Lord. Amen.

PRAYING THROUGH THE DAY

Grace Before Meals

Thanks be to Thee, O Lord, for these and all the blessings so generously provided. We thank Thee in the Name of Christ. Amen.

Lord, we thank Thee for this food. Sanctify it to our use, pardon our sins, and save us, for Christ's sake. Amen.

O God, Thy mercies are fresh every day and call forth each day anew our voices of thanksgiving. Through Jesus Christ. Amen.

We thank Thee, our Heavenly Father, for these Thy good gifts. Bless them to our use, strengthen us and keep us, for Christ's sake. Amen.

Our Father, we ask Thee to bless the food before us to our physical needs, and feed our spirits with Thy truth, for Jesus' sake. Amen.

PRAYING THROUGH THE DAY

Grace Before Meals

The strength of the hills, and the depth of the sea, the earth and its fulness belongeth to Thee; and yet to the lowly Thou bendest Thine ear, so ready their humble petitions to hear. Amen.

We are ever conscious, Lord, of our sinfulness and our constant need of Thee. Support our lives by Thy grace, and bring us safely to Thy heavenly home. Amen.

Let Thy blessing, Almighty God, descend on this portion of Thy bounty, and on us, Thy unworthy servants, through Jesus Christ our Lord. Amen.

Almighty God! the eyes of all wait upon Thee, and Thou givest them their meat in due season. Bless, we beseech Thee, the provisions of Thine earthly bounty, which are now before us; and let them nourish and strengthen our frail bodies, that we may the better serve Thee, through Jesus Christ. Amen.

PRAYING THROUGH THE DAY

Grace Before Meals

Cover all our sins with Thy pardon, O Christ, and make us strong to overcome all sins, especially the sin of ingratitude. In all these bounties help us to see Thee, and glorify Thee. Amen.

Bountiful Giver of every good and perfect gift! Thou art never weary of supplying our returning wants — grant, we pray Thee, that the food of which we are about to partake, may contribute to the comfort and support of our bodies, and enable us to engage with more zeal in Thy service. We ask it for Jesus Christ's sake. Amen.

Almighty God, we beseech Thee to pardon our sins: to bless the refreshment now before us, to our use, and us to Thy service, through Jesus Christ. Amen.

Thanks After Meals

Father of lights, from whom cometh down every good and perfect gift, enable us to receive these fruits of Thy bounty with humility and gratitude, and give us grace, that, whether we eat or drink, or whatever we do, we may do all to Thy glory. In Jesus' Name. Amen.

Bounteous God, we acknowledge our dependence on Thee, and our unworthiness of Thy benefits. We pray Thee to forgive our sins, to bless us in the reception of this food, and enable us to use the strength we may derive from it to Thy glory, for Christ's sake. Amen.

Sanctify, O Lord, we beseech Thee, these Thy provisions to our use, and us to Thy service, through Jesus Christ, our Lord. Amen.

**PRAYING THROUGH
THE DAY**

Thanks After Meals

We thank Thee, O God, our Heavenly Father, for the innumerable good gifts of Thy providence. Especially do we thank Thee for the rich provision Thou hast made for our souls — accept our grateful acknowledgments for the food we have now received; and enable us to prove our sincerity by the way we live, for the sake of our Lord and Saviour, Jesus Christ. Amen.

What shall we render to Thee, O God, for all Thy benefits? Every day of our lives we are receiving fresh tokens of Thy favor. Oh, let Thy goodness lead us to repentance. And if we can do no more than express our gratitude, help us to do that in the sincerity of our souls, and Thine shall be the glory, for ever, through Jesus Christ. Amen.

Thanks After Meals

Accept, Heavenly Father, our humble thanks for this and for all Thy blessings through Jesus Christ. Amen.

We thank Thee, our Heavenly Father, for the rich provision Thou hast made for our temporal and eternal welfare; especially for the food we have now received. May Thy goodness move us to thanksgiving, and Thy grace prepare us for our heavenly home, through Jesus Christ our Lord. Amen.

We praise Thee, O Lord, for the provisions of Thy providence and grace, and in particular for this renewed token of Thy favor. May we feel our increased obligations to live for Thee and be fitted at length to eat bread in Thy heavenly kingdom, through our Lord Jesus Christ. Amen.

**PRAYING THROUGH
THE DAY**

Thanks After Meals

We bless Thee, O Lord, for this kind refreshment. Be pleased to continue Thy favors, and feed us with the bread of life. Supply the wants of the needy, and enable us, while we live on Thy bounty, to live to Thy glory, for Christ's sake. Amen.

Blessed and praised be Thy holy Name, O Lord, for this and all Thy other blessings, bestowed upon us through Jesus Christ our Lord. Amen.

PRAYING THROUGH THE DAY

Evening and Bedtime Prayers

Eternal God, be our refuge, and protect us with Thine everlasting arms throughout the approaching night. We turn aside from the cares and duties of the fleeting day and look to Thee, O Lord, for rest. Thou hast said that Thou wilt give Thy beloved sleep. O God, may we arise from our slumbers to face the new day with renewed strength. May we ever follow Thee all the days of our life till we reach that land where Thou art the light, and night never comes. In Jesus' Name. Amen.

O Lord, we look to Thee for protection through the night. We know that Thou art able to keep us, for Thou wilt not slumber. Thou hast promised to preserve us from evil: Thou wilt also preserve our souls. Help us therefore to commit our way unto Thee, O Lord. We look to Thee to direct our paths. In Thy Name. Amen.

**PRAYING THROUGH
THE DAY**

Evening and Bedtime Prayers

O Lord, this glorious day has passed, and the evening time is here. May we invite Thee into our hearts as the disciples of old, "Abide with us, for it is evening and the day is far spent." Help us, O Lord, to relax after the perplexing problems of the day. Watch over us during the night and bring us to the new day with renewed spirit and blessed hope. In Thy Name. Amen.

Bedtime Prayers for Children

Now I lay me down to sleep,
I pray the Lord my soul to keep,
If I should die before I wake,
I pray the Lord my soul to take.

Jesus, tender Shepherd, hear me,
Bless Thy little child tonight.
Through the darkness, be Thou near me.
Keep me safe till morning light.

Prayers for Repentance and Confession

O God our Father, we come to Thee humbly confessing our sins and seeking Thy forgiveness. Thou alone hast the power to blot out our transgressions and to remember no more our sins against us. We claim nothing of ourselves. We rely only on Jesus Christ, Thy Son, our Saviour and Redeemer. Amen.

O Lord, teach us that the fear of the Lord is the beginning of wisdom. We read in Thy Word that nothing is hid which shall not be manifested. "He that covereth his sins shall not prosper; but whoso confesseth and forsaketh them shall have mercy." Help us to confess our faults fully and freely. Teach us the path of righteousness. For Thy Name's sake. Amen.

PRAYING IN
PUBLIC

Prayers for Repentance and Confession

Our most merciful Father, we have wandered away from the path of righteousness. We have followed, to our sorrow, our sinful desires. We have sinned against Thee. We have left undone many things which we should have done. Have mercy upon us, O God. According to Thy loving kindness have mercy upon us. Help us as we confess our sins; restore unto us the joy of Thy salvation; help us to know perfect peace. As we stay our minds upon Thee, grant, O merciful Father, that we may claim the promises of Thy Son, Jesus Christ our Lord, who said: "Him that cometh unto me I will in no wise cast out." In His Name. Amen.

Prayers for Repentance and Confession

We come to Thee, O God, in repentance. In the midst of Thy harmony how discordant is much of our life. We bring our poverty to Thee for Thy riches. We come to the River of Life for refreshment.

Help us to acknowledge our wrongdoing; help us to repent of specific sins in our lives. We need Thy great forgiveness; we need Thy great love; we must be nowhere else save in our Lord and Saviour Jesus Christ. Amen.

PRAYING IN PUBLIC

Prayers for Repentance and Confession

O Lord, we would not hide from ourselves and we may not hide from Thee the fact that we have sinned, that we have come short of Thy glory, that we have failed miserably in our own strength, but we know that Thou art Lord over all. We do not believe, O Lord, that there is even any battle between what we call sin and what we call goodness. We know that the battle has been fought and the victory won — won for us on Calvary. May we now, O Heavenly Father, rejoice that we are invited into the fellowship of His suffering, that we may be indeed His brethren and sisters. We ask in the Name of our Lord and Saviour, Jesus Christ. Amen.

PRAYING IN
PUBLIC

Prayers for Guidance

O precious Holy Spirit, help us to open the way for Thy presence. Thou art a Guide into all truth. Thou art a Comforter in all sorrow. Thou art also a Convictor of sin. Come into our hearts in all Thy fullness. Amen.

O God, we come to Thee for guidance. The flesh is so weak and the temptations are so many. Deliver us, O Father, from the snare of the enemy and make us vigilant, for our adversary is "As a roaring lion, walking about seeking whom he may devour." Guide us, O thou great Jehovah. Amen.

PRAYING IN PUBLIC

Prayers for Guidance

Come, Holy Spirit, come and endue our petitions with love and faith and hope. May we know that our Lord is helping us to pray, for we know so little. Our horizons are small and fade in the mist. Let this hour be an hour of prayer. All the way through this service may we be looking unto Thee, O God, and wilt Thou teach us how to pray. We ask in the Name of our Lord and Saviour, Jesus Christ. Amen.

O Lord God, our Heavenly Father, how stable and supreme is the thought that wherever, however we may have wandered, the Rock of Ages stands amid all the flood of things, bathed in the sunshine of love, cleft for each of us, a harbor and a haven. And we are here, O God, not to tell Thee in words, but to pray just now together that every heart here may be open to Thy message. Dear God, teach us how to pray in the Name of our Saviour, Jesus Christ. Amen.

Prayers for Guidance

O Lord God, we thank Thee that Thou followest us; Thou dost stand round about us; Thou dost beset us before and behind, because Thou dost love us. How often we forget Thee. Yet Thou hast not forgotten us. O Thou unforgetting love, lead us, nourish us, keep us safe. May this service be a blessing to each and every one. We ask in the Name of our Lord and Saviour, Jesus Christ. Amen.

Our eternal Father, who dost never forget us, who, though we are living in time, dost remind us of the eternity from which we come and into which we shall go — give our minds, we beseech Thee, the ability to grasp eternal truths just now. Exalt our spirits above earth, yet keep us faithful to the tasks at hand Thou hast given us to do. We pray this for Jesus Christ's sake. Amen.

PRAYING IN PUBLIC

Prayers for One's Country

O God, we pray Thee that we may hold our liberty in high esteem because Thou hast not dealt so with every nation. We thank Thee for this wonderful country in which we are privileged to live. Inspire all of our people to hold sacred this glorious heritage. Keep us from strife, and may we live together in unity. Keep us free from jealousy of race or class. Bless, we pray Thee, the President of our country. Give him Thy wisdom and strength. Be with all those in power. May the horrors of war soon pass forever from the earth and the Prince of Peace reign. Amen.

Prayers for One's Country

O God, the Father of our Lord Jesus Christ, the Great Shepherd of the sheep, who came to seek and to save the lost, we beseech Thee that Thy spirit may strive with those who, having strayed from Thy fold, are wandering in the wilderness of worldliness and sin. Let Thy love constrain them and Thy grace abound toward them, that they may return to Thee in penitence and fresh consecration of their lives.

Grant to us at this moment, O righteous Father, the spirit of worship and true godliness. Bind us together with cords of duty, making us glad and strong in doing it. By the memories of our Nation's glorious past, make us alert to the call of the present, that inspired by the spirit of wisdom, courage and patience we may respond with signal devotion to its just claims upon us.

We ask it in the Name of Him who hung upon the Cross, stretching forth His loving arms to draw all men unto Himself, Jesus Christ, Thy Son, our Lord. Amen.

PRAYING IN PUBLIC

Prayers for One's Country

O God, our Father, we pray for the Government of our country in these times of great peril. We beseech Thee, Thou God of all nations, to give us sobriety of judgment and a love for righteousness. Take away all fear that we may have for anything except that we may come short of Thy glory and Thy purpose. Let us fear Thee, O Lord, and help us to fear nothing else. Father, we pray Thee that in these moments when the children of men seem to be sundered one from another that some word may be spoken by Thy Holy Spirit in the silence between the battle shouts that shall grant unto all the world a new and lasting peace. We pray in the Name of our Lord and Saviour, Jesus Christ. Amen.

Prayers for the Afflicted

O God, Thou hast such tender care over us, even as a mother comforteth her children, Thou hast promised to comfort us. Graciously regard those who suffer affliction; visit them with Thy healing power. In Thy Name. Amen.

Each one of us personally brings to Thee nothing less than the problem of himself, and, O Lord, if we had not the grace of God stimulating us, strengthening us, guiding us, restraining us, we would not have been here praying for Thy love. We thank Thee for this grace of God. We pray for the pardon of our sins, for the purification of the Holy Spirit; we pray for all those, O Lord, to whom our hearts go in our sympathy and who have asked for an interest in our prayers, in the Name of our Lord and Saviour, Jesus Christ. Amen.

PRAYING IN
PUBLIC

Prayers for the Afflicted

O God of Mercy, we come to Thee in the interest of all the people. There are so many who turn aside from Thy will and way. Help us all to fix our thoughts and affections upon Thee. Amen.

O Thou most generous God, who seeth us in our afflictions and knowest our grief, we beseech Thee to take every bruised heart and heal it, to take every lame one and put him in the way of strength, to give sight to the blind and hope to the hearts of men. We pray in the Name of our Saviour, Jesus Christ. Amen.

Prayers for the Afflicted

O Lord, in our distress we call upon Thee, for Thou hast told us in Thy Holy Word to "call upon me in the day of trouble; I will deliver thee." Thou hast also said, "I will come and heal him." Have mercy on Thy servant who is ill. We thank Thee, our Father, for the skill of the doctors and nurses, and for the release Thou hast prepared through the skill of Thy servants. O Lord, all of the skill and remedies are in vain without Thy blessing. Restore the strength of this dear one who is ill. Bring us all at last into Thine Heavenly Kingdom. Amen.

O most merciful Father, grant to restore to health, we pray Thee, Thy servant. May those who administer unto him (her) be blessed in so doing. May all the means that are employed be used to the restoration of health to the body and mind. In Jesus' Name. Amen.

PRAYING IN
PUBLIC

Prayers for the Afflicted

O God of great mercy, we pray for those who are shut-in. Sustain them by the assurance of Thy presence. Lift them out of their despondency. May they have faith in Thee so that they may not become restless or discouraged. Give them the vision of the Cross-bearing Christ, who conquered pain and death. May the light of faith and hope radiate from his (her) room, as Thy promise is claimed: "The eternal God is thy refuge and underneath are the everlasting arms." Amen.

O God, by whose mercy we are surrounded in happy circumstances, help those who are poor and in need. While we have our joyous companionships and our friends and neighbors, let us not forget the fatherless, the friendless, the sick and the dying. Help them to realize that Thou art a friend to them and that Thou only hast the power to bring them unto a glorious life with Thee. Amen.

Prayers for the Afflicted

O Thou God who hast given unto us One of flesh and blood, who hast gone through the Valley of the Shadow of Death, we pray Thee this morning that Thine own great Servant, Thy Son, our Redeemer, shall go to bedsides of pain and sorrow and distress and lead our dear ones gently into the light of the day. We ask in the Name of our Lord and Saviour, Jesus Christ. Amen.

PRAYING IN
PUBLIC

Prayers for the Afflicted

We bring to Thee just now, Heavenly Father, those who have asked that we should pray for them, and we beseech Thee that though we do not know their name and Thou dost know all names, that Thou shalt find them by the feet of love and bless them and restore them. We pray Thee also, Heavenly Father, for those who are looking into the faces of them that seem to be dead and departed. May we know that death has no victory, may we understand that the grave has been despoiled of its triumph, and may they, above all, know that life has opened a new gateway and for him who so loved beauty may there be an abundant entrance into the land of Beauty and Truth, through Jesus Christ. Amen.

Prayers for the Afflicted

O Lord, we ask Thee, as we have been asked to pray that Thou shouldst go to the houses of mourning, that Thou shouldst give Thy great blessing to the sorrowing upon the earth. Lord, gather the most ragged, poorest, blindest, of Thy children in Thine arms of mercy. We ask this in the Name of Him who walked to the leper and cleansed him and gave sight to the eyes of the blind, our Saviour, Jesus Christ. Amen.

PRAYING IN
PUBLIC

Prayers for the Afflicted

O Lord, we are here today strangers to one another. Thou knowest us all together. We are here with many cares sending their roots down deep into sorrows and pains and betimes finding springs of joys. We are here with such a variety of experiences, and necessities numerous as they are that we make our appeal to the infinite God and pray Thee that this may be a place of blessing and forgiveness to all who come, and may the grace of the Lord go with us wherever we go; may we carry the light of joy of this communion and fellowship with us. We ask in the Name of our Lord and Saviour, Christ Jesus. Amen.

Prayers for the Armed Forces

O God, we ask that Thou wilt be with our soldiers. May they feel that they are supported by the God of Jacob. May they know that Thou art with them in the day of battle. In the day of peace help them to feel the Spirit of the Prince of Peace. May they serve with a faithful spirit. Give them great courage to serve their country as good servants. In Jesus' Name. Amen.

O God, Thou ruler of the universe, whose footsteps are upon the sea as well as upon the earth, we pray Thee to give Thine everlasting strength to all sailors of the sea. Preserve them from the dangers that lurk in the sea. May those gallant men who serve in the Navy and Marine Corps, and all others who serve on the sea, be ever faithful to this great country of ours. In Jesus' Name. Amen.

PRAYING IN
PUBLIC

Prayers of Devotion

"Where two or three are gathered together in my name, there am I in the midst of them." Dear Lord, these words come back to us over many ages, and we know that we are here in a building consecrated to Thy service, consecrated by Thy presence now and by Thy presence always to the worship of Almighty God. Wherever Thy children are, there is the temple of Thy Holy Spirit, and we pray Thee that in this place we may feel Thy presence with us. Here let us realize that the whole earth is Thy footstool, in the Name of Jesus Christ our Lord. Amen.

Prayers of Devotion

Our dear Saviour, we thank Thee that Thou hast chosen to call us friends and servants. Thou hast revealed unto us the secrets of Thy heart. Thou art a Friend that sticketh closer than a brother. Thou hast given Thyself for us. "Greater love hath no man than this, that a man lay down his life for his friends." We are so unworthy of such great honor. Thou art a refuge for all who have trouble and sorrow. Thou wilt supply our every need. May we come to Thee, our Saviour and Friend, whatever our need may be. Amen.

PRAYING IN
PUBLIC

Prayers of Devotion

O God, our God, God of all our life and of all our hope, our first thought just now is praise, and out of our praise there comes our prayer, haltingly enough, but sincerely, the prayer for light, the prayer for all the warmth that comes with the light. We thank Thee, O God, for the Light that is the light of men, for Him around whom we come, all our differences, with all our varied experiences united in one thing: that we do love Him and only Him — even Christ. O Lord, Thou knowest altogether what we would tell Thee if we could, and because Thou knowest and art all sympathetic and all powerful, we give this service into Thine own hands with our lives, our hearts, our hopes, in the Name of Jesus Christ, our Lord. Amen.

Prayers of Devotion

O Father, may we be endued with that love which is patient and kind. Take away from us all jealousy and rudeness. Cleanse our minds of selfishness. Give us a spirit of gladness which shall help us to bring gladness to others. In Thy Name. Amen.

Almighty Father, we rejoice in this truth: greater than all facts, mightier than all other impulses, sweeter than all other recollections is this — we belong to Thee. Much we have lost in life, much we have gained, but from the beginning and on and forever on, we are and shall be Thy children. Some of us have wondered, some of us have blundered — yea, all of us have made mistakes and sinned. Thou art our Father yet; Thou art our God yet, Thou art greater than evil, greater than sin. So we come to Thee. Receive us, we pray Thee, in the Name of our Lord and Saviour, Jesus Christ. Amen.

PRAYING IN PUBLIC

Prayers of Devotion

O dear Lord, we thank Thee for the Holy Scriptures which have been given unto us by Thine own inspiration. In Thy blessed Book we find help for our every need. In Thy Word we find hope and courage. Give us more of Thy grace so that we may feel Thy presence so real to us. In all of our difficult places in this life we have Thy promise, "My grace is sufficient for Thee." In Thy Name. Amen.

Almighty God, give us grace, that we may become like Thee. Thou hast promised to visit us even when two or three are gathered together in Thy Name. We bring our petitions to Thee, O Lord, claiming Thy promise. Visit us as we humbly profess Thy Name. Grant unto us a clearer understanding of Thy truth, so that we may walk in Thy way. We pray in Jesus' Name. Amen.

Prayers of Devotion

O God, the everlasting Lord and Father, who art with us in all our ways, we beseech Thee, as we bow our hearts in prayer, to fill us with the strengthening peace of Thy conscious Presence and with the knowledge that Thy love is at the root of everything. May we always place the value of the soul above the body, character above circumstance, and with simple, loving worship, by continual obedience to the call of duty, and by purifying ourselves, even as Thou art pure, may we come close to Thee. We ask it in the Name and for the sake of Jesus Christ, our Lord and Saviour. Amen.

PRAYING IN PUBLIC

Prayers of Devotion

Almighty God, our Father and Friend, we come before Thee with praise and thanksgiving. We are here because Thou art our Father. We draw aside from all Thou hast said to us in nature, from what Thou hast spoken to us in all the music in the fields and flowers and streams, to come into personal relationship with Thee. We are like children who wish more than Thy grace: we wish Thyself. We are like ones in a household where we would have Thy hand and smile and forgiveness, more than anything Thou canst give us. Give us these things today. We ask in the Name of our Lord and Saviour, Jesus Christ. Amen.

Prayers of Devotion

Almighty Father and Friend, command a blessing upon us, we beseech Thee, and let Thy blessing be Thine own presence, for without Thee we can do nothing. We are here because life is so important and heavy as a burden, and bright as a possibility glowing before us with its opportunities. Just because life is all these things and more than these things, we need our Father's hand and our Father's blessing and our Father's good leadership and guidance. We have come here, O Lord, to honor; we have come here with joy in our hearts; Thou wilt not disappoint us. Lead us, we beseech Thee, for Christ's dear sake. Amen.

O God, help us to be responsive to Thy will. Our hearts are so full of the many things that crowd out those of real worth. Open our eyes that we may see, our ears that we may hear and our lips that we may speak for Thee. May Thy spirit touch a responsiveness in our lives. Amen.

PRAYING IN PUBLIC

Prayers of Devotion

O Lord, with humble hearts we come into Thy presence. Help us to commit all of our ways unto Thee. Thou hast promised that if we come unto Thee we shall find rest in Thee. May we find rest from our troubles, sorrows and disappointments of this life. We thank Thee for the privilege of bringing everything to Thee in prayer, for Thou wilt never leave us comfortless. We rest solely on Thee, O Christ. Amen.

O Lord God, help us to find our rest in Thee. Give us the quietness, confidence and strength that cometh to all those who wait on Thee. In this world of tribulation Thou hast provided a haven of rest for all weary ones. May we ever remember that "there remaineth a rest to the people of God." In Thy Name. Amen.

A Prayer for a Newborn Child

Our most Gracious God, we thank Thee for this dear one whom the Scriptures call "the heritage of the Lord." We pray Thee that by precept and example he (or she) may have fellowship with Thee. Thou hast taught us that all who would attain unto salvation must humble themselves and become as "little children, for of such is the kingdom of God." May this little one be dedicated to Thee. O Christ, who took the children up into Thine arms, take this child and protect it by Thine own love and grace. Grant, O Saviour, that the parents may command their household to walk in Thy way; and that every member of the family may have faith, obedience and charity, and at last be given an abundant entrance into Thy holy family above. In Thy Name. Amen.

PRAYING IN PUBLIC

Prayers for Bereaved Families

Our dear Lord, we now call upon Thee because death has invaded the lives and homes of these dear ones. Thy Word tells us that "as one whom his mother comforteth, so will I comfort you." Help them to know that Thou art very near to them, "closer than hands or feet" in their sore need. Thou, O Christ, hast suffered so much that Thou hast been called the "man of sorrows, and acquainted with grief." We claim Thy promise, "I will not leave you comfortless; I will come to you." Give these dear ones the assurance that they "sorrow not without hope." Thou art "the resurrection and the life." Thou alone hast conquered death, and because Thou liveth we also shall live. In Thy Name. Amen.

Prayers for Bereaved Families

O God, our Father, Thou takest away, and who can hinder Thee, or say unto Thee, What doest Thou? Thou hast a right to do what Thou wilt with Thine own. Thou art Sovereign, and the reasons of Thy conduct are often far above, out of our sight; but Thy work is perfect, Thy ways past judgment. All Thy dispensations are wise, and righteous, and kind — kind, even when they seem to be severe.

Thou hast permitted death to invade our circle, and hast turned our dwelling into a house of mourning. May we find that it is better to be in the house of mourning than in the house of mirth. By the sadness of the countenance may the heart be made better, more serious to reflect, and more softened to take impression.

Now, unto Him that is able to keep us from falling, and to present us faultless before the presence of His glory, with exceeding joy, to the only wise God our Saviour, be glory and majesty, dominion and power, both now and ever. Amen.

PRAYING IN PUBRIC

Prayers for Forgiveness

Lord of All Power and Might, in whose hands are the lives of men and their true destiny: Grant unto us, Thy servants, the pardoning grace of Thy forgiveness, and cleanse us from our sins. Help us to realize more and more that, while man looketh on the outward appearance, God looketh on the heart, and that out of the abundance of the heart the mouth speaketh. We beseech Thee, therefore, so to purify our hearts that we may see clearly our own deepest need. Help us to behold the image of our God, and to grow up into His likeness. Through Jesus Christ our Lord. Amen.

O God, we pray that there may be a revival of spiritual living among us. May we be more concerned about the things that remain. Help us to catch a new vision of Christ, who will be ever present with all who open their hearts to Him. Amen.

Prayers for Forgiveness

Almighty God, our Father, who art holy, who lookest upon us, we come to Thee because Thou art holy. Have pity upon us, we beseech Thee. O God, restore unto us the joy of Thy salvation. We thank Thee for Calvary and what it meant and means today. Father, we thank Thee that we may come to that place as we do now and ask the forgiveness of our sins through Jesus Christ, our Lord. Amen.

Gracious Father, we thank Thee that Thou didst so love this world that Thou gavest Thine only Son, that whosoever believeth in Him should not perish but have everlasting life. Help us we pray Thee to "Behold the lamb of God, which taketh away the sin of the world." We come to Thee with repentance on our lips and in our hearts. Help us then to find pardon full and free, through Jesus Christ our Lord. Amen.

PRAYING IN
PUBLIC

PRAYERS FOR FORGIVENESS

O God, Thou art as a strong tower to those who trust in Thee. Help us to realize that Thou art able to keep us from falling. Give us the victory over those who would destroy our souls. May we be more than conquerors through Christ, who loves us. Amen.

O Blessed Christ, may we have cheerful hearts. Thou art a Saviour of good cheer. Help us to radiate cheerfulness in our daily walk and work. May we follow close to Thee. Increase our faith, so that after we have worked and given ourselves to Thee in prayer we may, with trusting hearts, commit all to Thee. We are assured that true joy comes to all who seek first of all Thy Kingdom. Amen.

Prayers for Forgiveness

O Lord, we pray Thee especially for Thy blessing upon us in the midst of all our life that we may learn to be patient with one another and learn to love one another deeply for Thy sake. Forgive us, we beseech Thee, O Lord, for hastiness, for irritability, for forgetfulness one of another, and may we so approach Thy mercy seat at this time that we shall know we have been taken into the beloved through our Lord and Saviour, Jesus Christ. In Jesus' Name. Amen.

PRAYING IN PUBLIC

Prayers of Worship and Thanksgiving

O Lord, how often we call to remembrance the former days and Thine infinite patience with us. Help us not to lose our victory now by casting away our confidence. Guard us against the evil of unbelief. We know that the secret of the Lord is with them that fear Him. Thou hast called us Thy friends. Thou art the same yesterday, today and forever. O gracious Lord, help us to look forward, remembering the recompense of the reward so soon to come and hold fast our confidence. Thou art the Author and Finisher of our faith and we will trust Thee till the end. In Thy Name. Amen.

PRAYERS OF WORSHIP AND THANKSGIVING

Our Heavenly Father, may we learn a lesson from the birds of the air, over whom Thou hast such tender care. May we not fret unduly over tomorrow, knowing that whatever befalls us, "The Lord is at hand." Help us to cast our every burden upon Thee, for Thou carest for us. Amen.

Our Father God, because we are Thy children, we are here, homeward bound, looking homeward because the feeling has been stirred within us in this first moment of worship that we belong to Thee and that Thou dost belong to us. We shall always be aweary and alien until we are in Thine own heart of hearts, reconciled by the love Thou hast given to the world in Jesus Christ, our Saviour. Father, we thank Thee for this hour. Let us open all the doors of gratitude that Thy mercy and guidance may come in. We will give Thee all the glory of this blessing through endless ages as we respond in our prayer unto Thee. Amen.

PRAYING IN PUBLIC

Prayers of Worship and Thanksgiving

Almighty God, we are in Thine own hands wherever we are, but especially do we feel the tender pressure of goodness as we come together to worship Thee, to see one another in the light of Thy great redemption. We thank Thee for the meanings of this hour, for the revelations of this moment as they come and go. We are more to one another because we are so much to Thee and Thou art so much to us. Seal these blessed friendships, unite our hearts in one constant theme and anthem of praise and prayer. May this morning be a morning indeed that shall invite into itself all the joys and hopes of Thy kingdom. We ask in the Name of our Lord and Saviour, Jesus Christ. Amen.

PRAYING IN PUBLIC

Prayers of Worship and Thanksgiving

O God, we do not know what we should ask of Thee, for our failures are many. Fill our hearts with Thy goodness. Give us strength to overcome the temptations of this life. Endue us with Thy Spirit, so that we will live better lives. May the community in which we live be enriched because we walk close to Thee. In Jesus' Name. Amen.

O God, help us to remember that we should practice humility. We know that this is the way our Saviour taught us. May we never be provoked by wrath, but ever keep before us His life as our example, who, when He was reviled, reviled not again. Amen.

PRAYING IN
PUBLIC

Prayers of Worship and Thanksgiving

Almighty God, who art our Father, in whose Name we have the expectation of grace because Thou hast said, "For my Name's sake will I do this, will I redeem thee, will I comfort thee, will I save thee," hear us, we beseech Thee, as we come into Thy presence and not relying upon our own selves but relying upon our God, seeking and finding peace and satisfaction by Thy grace, in Jesus Christ. Forgive our failures and shortcomings and, above all, all our sins. We ask in the Name of our Lord and Saviour, Jesus Christ. Amen.

It is our confession, our Heavenly Father, and it is our joy to remember that while we are praising Thee here below there is an anthem above, and when we think of what is above us and those who have been dear to us who have passed on, we join with the heavenly host and say, "Praise God from whom all blessings flow."

Prayers of Worship and Thanksgiving

How they have been flowing for these many years into all our lives! How many times we have mistaken the meaning of these blessings; how often we have not called them blessings at all — but "Praise God from whom all blessings flow" that the blessings still are flowing; that it has made no difference with our Heavenly Father's bounty that we have counted it a little thing. Oh, forgive us, gracious God, that we have ever underestimated; that we have missed in appreciation the divine Gift. And give us one more gift this morning: Thy perpetual blessings, and especially as we worship here bring our lives into the great Repair Shop of Thy love as we bring our foolishness and our sin and our needs, along with the better things.

Oh, give us Thyself, the presence of Thyself, and all will be well, in Jesus' Name. Amen.

**PRAYING ON
SPECIAL DAYS**

Christmas

Almighty God, the Father of our Lord Jesus Christ, we humbly beseech Thee to accept our thanks for the manifold mercies which Thou hast poured upon us.

We bless Thee, especially, for sending Thy well-beloved Son, to take our nature upon Him, and to be made in the likeness of sinful flesh.

We rejoice that unto us a Child is born; that unto us a Son is given. And we would join the multitude of the heavenly host, in ascribing glory to Thee in the highest; peace on earth; good will toward men.

We praise Thee for revealing to us the way in which mercy and truth have met together; in which righteousness and peace have kissed each other. And we account it a faithful saying, and worthy of all acceptation, that Christ Jesus came into the world to save sinners.

Vouchsafe, O Lord, Thy special blessing to us this day.

CHRISTMAS

Have compassion, also, on those who have never heard of the coming of our blessed Lord in the flesh. In Him who hath arisen to rule over the Gentiles, let the Gentiles trust, and find His rest to be glorious.

Mercifully with Thy favor look upon the whole Christian world. May all that name the name of Christ depart from iniquity. Especially preserve them from turning this season into an occasion of revellings and unholy mirth. Let them rejoice, as Christians, in Christ their Saviour; and let Thy grace teach them to deny all ungodliness and worldly lusts, and to live soberly, righteously and godly, in this present world. In Jesus' Name. Amen.

**PRAYING ON
SPECIAL DAYS**

Christmas

O Lord, we do praise Thee. In this Christmas light we give Thee the adoration of our hearts, and we pray Thee that we may give to Thee the loyalty of our lives. O Thou Gift of gifts opening a new world, making the whole universe radiant with Thy presence, be Thou with us this morning; be Thou with us through all our life, with all the benefits of the gospel of Love and with all the benevolences of the Spirit of God, and especially be Thou with us, O Lord, throughout our life with Thy grace. May we not merely be glad; may we be obedient, obedient to all the light of Christmas, so that now we shall open our hearts and make our hearts a Christmas gift indeed, in the Name of our Lord and Saviour, Jesus Christ. Amen.

PRAYING ON SPECIAL DAYS

CHRISTMAS

Almighty God, we thank Thee for Thine only Son, Jesus, the only begotten of the Father, who took upon Himself our flesh, thus becoming one of us. We deplore our fearful condition that necessitated the giving of Thy Son for our sins. Help us to live for Thee on earth, and may every day be as joyous as the day of Christmas. In Jesus' Name. Amen.

O God, help us to remember that the dear Lord Jesus came to earth and dwelt among us. He is indeed Emmanuel, "God with us." Then if Thou be with us we need not fear, for Thou art more than all that can come against us. Fill our hearts with great confidence and hope. For the Redeemer's sake. Amen.

**PRAYING ON
SPECIAL DAYS**

New Year's Day

Our Father, we have passed the threshold of another year. We realize how miserably we have failed to attain the goal which we set before us a year ago. Help us, O God, to press toward the mark of the high calling in Christ Jesus our Lord this year. In all of our failures of the past year Thou hast been so patient with us. Thou art so merciful. Grant to us this year the faith to live the life of a Christian, and may we seek first of all Thy Kingdom and its righteousness. May our highest ambition be to know Thee more fully and to follow in Thy footsteps. In Jesus' Name. Amen.

PRAYING ON SPECIAL DAYS

New Year's Day

Almighty and everlasting God, our Heavenly Father, Thou who hast been our refuge from one generation to another and in whose sight a thousand years are but as yesterday, seeing that is past as a watch in the night, grant to us Thy children at this the dawn of another year grace to meet each day.

If in the coming days Thou wouldst have us walk betimes with sorrow when the hosannas of our home are hushed with loved ones gathered to their rest, when the palm trees of life's garden are withered and all our days are dread; then comfort us with the thought that as the wind speaks not more sweetly to the giant oaks than to the least of all the blades of grass, so he alone is great who turns the voice of sorrow into a song made sweet by the whisper of Thy love.

All of this we ask in the Name and for the sake of Jesus Christ our Lord. Amen.

**PRAYING ON
SPECIAL DAYS**

New Year's Day

O Thou God of Eternity, we come to Thee who dost behold the sands of time and dost know our frame. Deepen in us, we pray Thee, this morning the sense of Eternity. Let us know, O God, from above, by some whisper out of the Eternal, the meaning of Time. May we realize that we are of yesterday, but that the eternal tomorrow stretches before us. To the God of eternity may we give all the glory of our New Year's praise and prayer, in the Name of our Lord and Saviour, Jesus Christ. Amen.

PALM SUNDAY

Our Heavenly Father, Thou hast created us and redeemed us. Thou knowest us altogether; Thou knowest all of us. We come to Thee this morning in the Name of Him who died for us and rose again.

May we be prepared especially this morning for the days that are to come, that we may enter the gates of that Easter Morning again with thanksgiving, as we may enter the gates of heaven with joy! We thank Thee, Lord, that "surely Thou hast borne our griefs and carried our sorrows," Thou Christ of God! Help us to live as if we believed this tremendous truth. In Jesus' Name. Amen.

**PRAYING ON
SPECIAL DAYS**

Good Friday

Our Lord Jesus, we rejoice in the fact that Thou didst bear the Cross up Calvary Hill for us. We see Thee lifted up on that Cross, and we feel the magnetic drawing toward Thee and the Cross. Draw us, O Christ, away from the sinful unto Thyself. Help us to be faithful to Thee until death removes us from the scenes of earth. Until then, help us, O Christ, to cherish Thy Cross and what it means to us. And then at the last may we hold Thy Cross before our closing eyes, until we open them in the glorious place Thou hast prepared for us. In Thy Name. Amen.

Easter

O God, we thank Thee for the comforting assurance of the fact that we shall live with Thee. Thou hast promised to redeem us from death: "O death, where is thy sting; O grave, where is thy victory?" "But now is Christ risen from the dead and become the firstfruits of them that slept." May we have a place with Thee in that great company of the redeemed. In our Redeemer's Name. Amen.

O God, we thank Thee for the provision Thou hast made for our salvation, even the giving of Thy Son, who suffered death on the Cross for us. We rejoice in the fact of the resurrection. Give us grace that we may follow in the Saviour's footsteps, dying daily to sin, that we may live evermore with Him. In our Saviour's Name. Amen.

**PRAYING ON
SPECIAL DAYS**

EASTER

O Thou who art the Resurrection and the Life, we give Thee the honor and joy, the loyalty and love of our hearts this morning. We come to the end of the grave today, O Thou ascended Christ, and find the Gospel — good news of hope for those who are hopeless, the news of a life beyond for those whose lives here have failed, the news of the song round about the throne, sung by the redeemed, who have redemption in our Lord and Saviour, Jesus Christ.

O Thou mighty Christ, Thou who didst burst asunder the bonds of death, Thou who hast the keys of hell and of death, accept our praise and thanksgiving. We thank Thee for our victory in Thee. In the name of our victorious Lord. Amen.

PRAYING ON SPECIAL DAYS

Easter

O Lord, we pray Thee today that this may be a day of comfort and sweetness, especially to those who know the sorrow and loss which comes by death. We would not make less, we would not make more painful the fact that we have known death. Thou hast spoken to us. Thou hast taken leaders from their places of power, and O Thou hast also spoken in the cottage and hamlet away out yonder on the plain, in the loneliness of the night. Thou hast sent Thine angel called death up and down the streets of our life, and this angel has not made a difference with the rich and poor. Send Thou Thine angel of life, and may every household and every lonely heart today feel and know the joy and persuasion of Easter. We ask in the Name of Him who was the Resurrection and is the Life. Amen.

**PRAYING ON
SPECIAL DAYS**

Easter

O Ascended Christ, we pray this morning as to a friend. We do not believe that any distances between those we love and our lives should call for cessation of prayer or praise. We speak this morning, O Lord, out of the stricken heart of humanity, and we pray Thee to stretch the scarred hand of Thy sacrifice over all the darkness and tumult of the times, and to give us this blessing in the Name of our Lord and Saviour, Jesus Christ. Amen.

Easter

"Surely, He has borne our griefs and carried our sorrows."

We add to our prayers, O God, the thanksgiving of our hearts that we have found such a pathway as this to the everlasting Burden-bearer. We thank Thee, our Father, that the Lamb that was slain from the foundation of the world is the testimony to the fact that Thou hast put Thine own strength under our burden. We rejoice in the tenderness with which Thou hast carried this burden in the person of our Saviour.

Make us grateful men and women this morning, that above everything else Thou hast borne our iniquities and below all else in uttermost darkness Thou art carrying our burden. Make our lives sacred this morning by the help and influence of Him who died, that we might have life and life more abundantly, even Jesus Christ, our Lord. Amen.

PRAYING ON
SPECIAL DAYS

Mother's Day

Speak to us, Thou Still Small Voice, as we await Thy message. Many of us are here on this day dedicated to "Mother." We are here with mother, and we thank Thee and speak with the still, small voice, as a mother comforteth her children. Others of us are here with experiences of motherhood. They yet abide, these angels of our childhood, and bend over us. Speak to us as our mother spoke to us the dearest things — all great things — in a still, small voice.

We are here, all of us, children of hope. Help us so to live as to be worthy, and, O Lord, help us, above all, to lift one humble prayer this morning for the mothers of the land. Speak and teach them to speak to their children in a still, small voice — not the tempest, not the earthquake, not the fire. So help these mothers of the land to bring out of all the tumult and discord, the noise of our time, the music of the inner life and the inner hope.

We ask in the Name of Him who has spoken to us, even Jesus. Amen.

Memorial Day

Almighty God, we thank Thee for our country, the land of the Stars and Stripes. May our flag ever keep waving in heavenly breezes. May we have grateful patriotism; may it be rooted in the bedrock of gratitude with deep devotion to the institutions and high ideals of which our country's flag is an emblem. Help us to so consecrate ourselves to the great heritage of freedom that it shall be a never failing light. In Jesus' Name. Amen.

**PRAYING ON
SPECIAL DAYS**

Memorial Day

We ask Thy blessing this morning, O God, upon the nation that walks with stately and solemn step to bedew with tears again the flowers that grow out of the graves of our fallen warriors. We thank Thee, our Father, for a clean flag. We pray Thee that we may help to keep it clean by being right and just and heroic for truth. We beseech Thee, O Lord, to lead with Thine own tender hand these our old soldiers who remain today to reflect glory upon our shield. Lead them with infinite tenderness. May their sleep be postponed until our nation shall be wakened to the greatness of the truths for which they fought and in whose glory they shall stand. We ask in the Name of our Lord and Saviour, Jesus Christ. Amen.

Fourth of July

O Lord, in an age when we are likely to be attracted by things instead of thoughts, may we look to the scarred face on Calvary to see molded the mighty leaders of our modern manhood.

Forgive us our sins as American citizens, that we have not recognized the value of those simple and superb virtues which come back today with the recollection of more than one hundred years. Forgive us, our Father, that we have forgotten our duties of men in a republic, the duties of men and women in the new dawning democracy, the new duties that need to be performed. Forgive us through Thy blessing from on high on the whole nation today. Guard the life of the President of the United States; guard and guide him and all others in authority by Thy gracious love. Give us, we beseech Thee, today the realization of the enormous responsibility of power, and help us in all the activities of education and

**PRAYING ON
SPECIAL DAYS**

Fourth of July

charity, that each man may feel his own responsibility as in the olden times. May every man before his own doorway make the pathway safe, and may every man by his own gathering of the manna in the morning-time have the fresh inspiration of divine grace in the Leader of all men and the Master of all men, even Jesus. Amen.

Labor Day

In the Name of our great Burden-bearer, our Saviour, Jesus Christ, we come into Thy presence, our Heavenly Father. We thank Thee for this day dedicated to the cessation of labor for a time, dedicated to all those who find joy in working the works Thou hast given them to do. Help us, our Father, to be truly grateful for our privileges and responsibilities. And help us, too, to do all as unto Thee. We pray in Jesus' Name. Amen.

Thanksgiving

Our Father, Thou hast abundantly blessed this earth on which we live with great harvests. Thou hast provided for mankind all things needful. Bless those who labor in the fields. May we ever rejoice in Thy great goodness to us. Help us to forget not all Thy benefits. This is a good land in which we live. On this day of Thanksgiving we thank Thee for our food, our schools, books and many churches. Above all we thank Thee for Thy Son, Jesus. May the words of the Psalmist be our prayer: "Bless the Lord, O my soul: and all that is within me, bless his holy name." Amen.

PRAYING ON
SPECIAL OCCASIONS

For Youth

Almighty God, we pray Thy blessing upon our schools, colleges and all of our institutions of learning. May the teachers possess a keen appreciation of their great opportunity to help the youth of our country to make the most of their mentality. May the youth understand that education is not complete unless pursued in the school of God as well as in the school of the world.

Thou hast taught us in Thy Word that whatsoever things are true, just, honest, pure, lovely and of good report; if there be any virtue, and if there be any praise, we should think on these things. Reveal unto the youth Thy truth, "The fear of the Lord is the beginning of wisdom." "This wisdom is a defence, . . . but the excellency of knowledge is that wisdom giveth life to them that hath it." O Lord, open Thou our eyes that we may behold wondrous things in Thy law. In Jesus' Name. Amen.

**PRAYING ON
SPECIAL OCCASIONS**

For a Sick Child

O God of the spirits of all flesh, the only giver and preserver of life in every living soul; the smallest, as well as the greatest, are Thy work and Thy care; and neither is without the compass of Thy providence, nor below the notice and regard of our heavenly Father, who, though so great above all, yet despiseth not any! O Lord, let Thy thoughts be full of pity and tender mercy to this poor sick child, for whose afflictions we are now concerned; and send him that relief and comfort from the load, or increase the strength to bear it; and deal gently and graciously with him, O Lord, beyond what we are worthy to ask at Thy hands, even for Thy own goodness' and mercy's sake. Amen.

**PRAYING ON
SPECIAL OCCASIONS**

For Peace

O Lord, because Thou hast manifested and expressed Thine own nature in Jesus Christ, because looking through the Son we see the Father and we know the Father is manifested in the Son, we bring to Thee again the memory of the fact that our earth is stained and stricken with war. O Lord, we pray Thee that by Thy power war shall cease. Wilt Thou lead men and women to the consideration of the command of our Lord, Jesus Christ; may we hear over the storm of battle and shriek of shell the Voice saying, "Peace I give unto you. My Peace I give to you. Let not your heart be troubled, neither let it be afraid." We ask in the Name of our Lord and Saviour, Jesus Christ. Amen.

PRAYING ON SPECIAL OCCASIONS

For Peace

O God, who hast made of one blood all nations of men to dwell on the face of the earth, who in Thy Holy Word hast taught us that One is our Father, that we all are brethren, we pray Thee in this dark hour of international strife that Thou wilt open the eyes of Thy people, those who in Thy Name are entrusted with the authority of government to see and understand their right and true relation to Thee and through Thee to one another. Teach them that hatred and violence are not strength, but weakness; that the true safeguarding of a nation is not to be found in weapons of war, but in these eternal principles which make for truth and brotherhood. Give to those who shall suffer in the war which is now raging the consolations of Thy grace; heal the sick and comfort the wounded; minister to the dying and bind

**PRAYING ON
SPECIAL OCCASIONS**

For Peace

up the broken heart. Bring, we pray Thee, to a speedy end this international battle, and hasten, we pray Thee, the time when peace shall flourish out of the earth and all shall dwell together in unity and love and war shall be no more. We ask it in the Name of our Saviour, Jesus Christ. Amen.

O God, we pray for the coming of Thy kingdom on the earth. Of that day and hour we know not, but we know that Thou wilt come according to Thy promise. Thy name is the Prince of Peace. We pray Thee to help us cast out all of the evil in our heart that gives cause for war. Thou loving Prince of Peace, remove from us all hatred and sinful desires. May Thy spirit direct our aims and ambitions. May we walk with Thee in pleasant ways and paths of peace. In Jesus' Name. Amen.

**PRAYING ON
SPECIAL OCCASIONS**

For Peace

O God, grant unto us Thy peace. Thou hast promised to give us perfect peace if we trust in Thee. Even though we live in a world of tribulations, we are not fearful and afraid. Thy Son our Saviour said, "I have overcome the world; my peace I give unto you." Give us, we pray Thee, this peace. In His Name. Amen.

For Love

O Father, we thank Thee that Thou hast revealed Thyself to us as a God of love. Our finite minds cannot fathom Thine infinite love, that while we were yet sinners Thou gavest Thine only Son to die for our sins. Give us the love that is kind, patient, pure and rejoiceth in truth. O Father, whatever changes may come to us in this changing world, Thy love never faileth. In Thy Name. Amen.

**PRAYING ON
SPECIAL OCCASIONS**

For a Newly Married Couple

Most Gracious Saviour, bless, we pray, these two who have just pledged themselves to each other in the bonds of Holy Matrimony. This, O Lord, is honorable, and signifies the union that exists between Thee and Thy Church. It was upon an occasion such as this which Thou didst adorn and beautify with Thine own presence and first miracle in Cana of Galilee. We pray that the love of these two may be strong, holy and deathless. May they soberly see beyond these precious days to the future. Grant that they may regard their home to be a sacred sanctuary, in which Thou, O Christ, shalt find Thy place as the Head of the family. In Thy Name. Amen.

**PRAYING AS A
SUNDAY SCHOOL TEACHER**

Blessed Lord, Thy touch is what we need to heal the fever of our selfish passions and free us from the disease of sin. And Thy touch hath still its ancient power. Therefore let it be felt by many today, and may some in this place find salvation from sin today. May the Gospel go out in the power of Thy Spirit to all people and a great turning to Christ take place even where the powers of evil are mightiest. To that end strengthen, guide and use all faithful missionaries, preachers and teachers of Thy Word. Purify Thy Church from worldliness, love of ease and indifference to sin and need. Restore to every Christian heart a warm devotion to Christ, and lead us all into those words and ways of Christian

PRAYING AS A
SUNDAY SCHOOL TEACHER

As a Church Worker

witness, those ministries of love and mercy by which we best shall honor Thee and bless others. Where people are downcast, disappointed, distressed and suffering, bring Thy servants to serve their need, and let the day soon dawn when sin shall be vanquished forever and sorrow and sighing shall flee away. Hear us, forgiving all our sins, for our blessed Saviour's sake. Amen.*

---

* The prayers in this section are taken from "The Sunday School Times."

PRAYING AS A SUNDAY SCHOOL TEACHER

Holy and merciful Father, whose Word is a lamp unto our feet, a light to our pathway through a darkly sinful world, we thank Thee that again we may together open Thy Book and ponder its teachings. Help us both to understand what we read and to obey it in our daily life. Forgive us our transgressing of Thy commands and break in us every evil habit, that we may live more like our Lord and Saviour. Bless with revival Thy whole Church on earth. Girdle the globe with the Gospel and bring sinners to Christ and salvation in every place. Overthrow the power of Satan and bring in the Kingdom of our Lord. Help and comfort those who are sick, the ill-treated, the needy and the sad. Show us our duty in the face of the human need that we encounter, and help us to be channels of Thy mercy to many. Through this new week grant us Thy guarding, guiding presence and the joy of the Lord as our strength, for our Saviour's sake and glory. Amen.

**PRAYING AS A
SUNDAY SCHOOL TEACHER**

Holy and merciful Father, whose hatred of sin and love of souls moved Thee to send the Lord Jesus to be our Saviour, we thank Thee for Him and for Thy love in giving Him even to the death of the Cross. As we, each one, look by faith at His Cross this day, we pray, "Help me walk from day to day with its shadow o'er me." For the world is ever near to lure us with its tainted attractions. Make the Lord Jesus to be everything to us, that love of sin and self and the world may die in us. Guide our study just now and bless Thy Word to all who hear it today. Use Thy faithful servants everywhere to draw many to Christ. Hasten the time when all shall own His rule. Lift up the fallen, cheer the faint, heal the sick and move all who are in trouble to seek Thee and find Thy help and comfort. Forgive our sins, renew a right spirit within us, and lead us in paths of upright and helpful living always, for the sake of Thy dear Son, our Lord. Amen.

PRAYING AS A SUNDAY SCHOOL TEACHER

Our holy, Heavenly Father, whose ear is open to Thy people's cry, we thank Thee for all blessings received in answer to prayer. Forgive us when we pray without heart and sincerity, when prayer is mere words. Show us our needs, needs of our dear ones, of our church, our land and the world so that we may be driven to our knees. Set all Thy people praying and answer abundantly beyond what they ask, to the praise of Thy Name and the deliverance of our needy world. Oh, that Thy Name might be hallowed, Thy Kingdom come, and Thy will be done here on earth, as we are taught to pray. Remember today all who are hard pressed by want, sickness, or any earthly woe. Draw out their faith to Thyself, cheer their spirits, and work out Thy best for each one. Bless our study of Thy Word now and keep and guide us through this week that our lives may serve Thy will and bring honor to our Saviour. Amen.

PRAYING AS A YOUTH LEADER

O God, our Heavenly Father, we thank Thee that Thou didst speak through the Apostle Paul when Thou didst say in Thy Word to Timothy, "Let no man despise thy youth." We thank Thee that as young people bought with a price, the precious blood of Jesus, we can approach Thy throne of grace, confident that Thou dost hear and answer the prayers of Thy blood-bought children. We ask Thee, Lord, to bless us as we gather here, to direct our thoughts and activities. Bless those who will minister to us. In our Saviour's Name we pray. Amen.

PRAYING AS A YOUTH LEADER

Our Father God, in the Name of Thy Son, our Saviour, we come to Thee in prayer. We are thankful that Thou didst welcome even the children, saying, "Suffer the little children to come unto me, and forbid them not." As Christian young people, washed white in the blood of the Lamb, we lay before Thee our petitions and praise. Be in our midst in this meeting, Lord, and meet the need of every heart. Be with those of our group who are absent from us for reasons of health or otherwise. Visit them with Thy presence and power. Endow our speaker and those who bring us special numbers in song with Thy grace that they may bring Thy message for our hearts today. In Jesus' Name. Amen.

PRAYING AS A
YOUTH LEADER

We never cease to be amazed, our Heavenly Father, that Thou didst love us, sinful as we are, enough to send Thine only Son to die for us. We pray Thy forgiveness, Lord, for our own thoughtlessness as young people, our carelessness about spiritual things. May our gathering today be a means of drawing us closer to Thee, and guiding us into a more circumspect walk that those about us might "take knowledge of (us) that (we) have been with Jesus." Help us to consecrate our lives in Thy service. "Thou hast done great things for us, whereof we are glad." May we radiate this gladness to others. In our Saviour's Name we pray. Amen.

"O God, our help in ages past, Our hope for years to come," meet with us today as we gather in this place to consider Thee and Thy majesty. Make us conscious that we as Christian young people need to be much in prayer that we might overcome and be victorious Christians, "meet for the Master's service." Help us by Thy grace so to live as to reflect honor and glory unto Thy Name, and to attract other young people. Speak to us through Thy servant that we may go forth from here strengthened in our inner man. In our blessed Saviour's Name. Amen.

PRAYING AS A PASTOR

INVOCATIONS*

O God, Thou source of all mercy, give us the assurance that we are not only in Thy house but in Thy presence. Humbled by the consciousness of our past infirmities —our thoughtless lives, our impatient tempers and our selfish aims, we come to Thee for mercy and forgiveness. We are filled with shame as we think of the numerous times that we have defaced Thine image, grieved Thy spirit and strayed from Thy ways. But in the midst of it all Thou hast opened for us a new and living way into the highest, the holiest and the best; but we feel that we cannot enter it until Thou hast graciously spoken to us the word of pardon. Be pleased to do so, and with it grant us the single eye, the believing mind, the grateful heart, the receptive nature and the brave and heroic spirit. Grant us grace to open the avenues of the mind

* These invocations are taken from the pen of W. G. Davis.

Invocations

and the gateways of the soul to Thy light and truth, to Thy love and pity. Show us that our joy is in Thy strength, and our peace in the consciousness of Thy presence. Impart to our littleness Thine almightiness and invade our loneliness with heaven's richest and choicest benediction. This prayer we offer in that Name to which every knee shall bow and every tongue confess. Amen.

O God, through Thine infinite goodness, we find ourselves once more in Zion, and before Thee. Show us the attitude we must assume, and the spirit we must exhibit while together, in order to profit by this service. Be pleased to deliver us from the delusion of self-complacency, from the desire to parade before Thee our attainments and achievements, and from our proneness to compare our sayings and doings with those of others.

We would stand before Thee just as we are; we would plead nothing save Thy

INVOCATIONS

wonderful compassion, and the rich promises of Thy Son, our Saviour. We would consider ourselves in the light of His Cross. We would see and feel our sin — its power, its guilt, its deception. Give us, we entreat of Thee, spiritual discernment to see it as Thou seest it, and above all, grant us grace to loathe it, to confess and forsake it.

Speak the tender word of forgiveness in response to our penitence, and clothe us with the robe of Christ's righteousness, then we shall go to our homes feeling that there is no condemnation to them who walk not after the flesh but after the spirit. Graciously hear and answer our prayer in the Name of Jesus. Amen.

For Thine unfailing mercy, Heavenly Father, which encircles our lives, and never forgets, we lift to Thee the song of praise, and the tribute of a thankful heart. We bless Thee for this holy contagion, for this celestial exercise of uniting song with song, and prayer with prayer, in sweet and filial

Invocations

affection of our loyalty and indebtedness to Thee. Show us, we pray Thee, in response to our trust, Thy willingness to give us such a blessing that no song can fully interpret, and no words can adequately express. To this end help us to slip out of our littleness, and narrowness, and self-absorption, into Thine infinitude, and into those larger and richer fields of devotion and service that are the portion of the pure in heart and merciful in spirit. May we see that we can best magnify Thy Name in being organs of truth, heralds of mercy and channels of everything lovely and helpful. May this union and concert mark our worship and characterize our service, then we shall have a greater desire than ever to taste the upper springs of Thy good pleasure, and realize once more that the glory of our strength, and the permanence of our riches, and the safety of our souls must be in Thee. Hear this, our prayer, through Jesus Christ, our Lord. Amen.

PRAYING AS A
PASTOR

INVOCATIONS

With voices full of praise and with hearts stirred with rapturous emotion, we draw near to Thee, our Father and our God. While grateful for all Thy gifts we are specially thankful for the sure and blessed hope of an endless life through the resurrection of our Lord and Saviour Jesus Christ. Well may we break forth into ecstatic joy as we remember the sting that has been taken out of death, and the victory that has been captured from the grave. Well may we comfort ourselves as we recall the joy that the risen Lord kindled in hearts where hope had well-nigh gone. Well may we rejoice and be glad on this festive morn as we think of the greatness of His work in conquering our last enemy, and in opening to us such a glorious inheritance. Help us to keep this blessed estate ever before us, and to rise day by day in song, in aspiration, and holy endeavor to its exalted life. To this end may we set our affections upon it, and covet its best

Invocations

gifts, and ever open our hearts to receive its legacy of peace. May we feel today more grateful than ever that the time will come when there will be no cloud in our sky, and no tear in our eye, no pang in our heart, and no barrier in our way because of our Lord's victory over death and the tomb. Amen.

O Thou, who dwellest in light to which none can approach, suffer us to come as near to Thee as the weakness and limitations of our mortality will allow. Thou dost condescend to come to our level, we could never rise to Thine. Lift us into a more refreshing atmosphere, and to that altitude from which we shall see something more of the glory of Thy nature and the significance of Thy Kingdom. Give us an insight into our deepest need. We have given away our hearts for sordid food; we have spent our strength for that which yields no profit, we have parted with our money for that which was not bread, and we have squan-

INVOCATIONS

dered the treasure of our life for things which were of no account. We now turn to Thee, and pray that Thou wouldst reveal to us the life worth living, the work worth doing and the cause worth maintaining. Show us that all other service is worthless and profitless in comparison with Thine. May our ambition in life be worthy of Thee and of Thy Church; may our sense of obligation and loyalty to Thee, and to truth, be as irresistible as fire, strong as steel, and firm as a rock. Let Thy peace rest upon every person now before Thee, and hear Thou in Heaven the individual cry of each one of us in the name of our once crucified and now risen and exalted Lord. Amen.

O Thou, who comprehendest all time, and who art from everlasting to everlasting, we come to Thee. For the illuminating and unerring chart which Thou hast given us in Thy Word we thank Thee. Help us to see more vividly, and to feel more deeply

INVOCATIONS

that it is the one Book that we need more than any other. May our chief delight be found in becoming better acquainted with it. Grant that its teaching may pervade our whole life, purifying our thoughts and controlling all our actions. May all our decisions be settled by its standards, and all our enterprises carried on according to its authority. Hasten the time when it will be more profoundly revered and more diligently read, when it will occupy in every mind, in every home, in every land, the position that it occupies in this church and at this service. May we have such a vision of its importance that ere we leave we shall pray, as never before, that it will be the first book in our possession, then its light will illumine our understanding and banish from it all false conceptions, and every possible illusion. This we ask in the Name of Him who is the Way, the Truth and the Life. Amen.

PRAYING AS A PASTOR

Prayers of Worship and Dedication

Kind and loving Father, we are poor and shortsighted, needing guidance, and particularly when we draw near to Thee in prayer. We can only confess our sins, and bring our wants before Thee as we are taught by Thy Spirit. We bless Thee for this Thy latest gift — the gift of this day, and for its accompanying favors, health and strength to enjoy it, in the best of all places, at Thy feet and in Thy presence. May we be fully established in Thy love and power, and be ever strengthened and encouraged by the assurance of Thy goodness and grace. Show us that Thy Presence in our midst is not to fill us with fear, but to inspire us to live better, to pray more fervently, and to work with greater zeal. May the message of Thy grace shine through our imperfect speech and fall upon attentive ears and receptive hearts. May the varied gifts with which we are endowed be used with a consecration, and with a directness in all we attempt for Thee.

PRAYING AS A PASTOR

Prayers of Worship and Dedication

But above all may there be in us a strong attachment to Jesus Christ, and may there be a blessed contagion about our love to Him that will spread as we come in contact with others, through Jesus Christ our Lord. Amen.

O Thou, who art the Fountain of all life, and the Disposer of all destinies, for whom no dawn arises and no evening sets, we draw near to Thee. Day and night, time and eternity, are alike unto Thee. We thank Thee for the wonderful provision which Thou hast made for our physical refreshment and spiritual renewal. For the rest of the past night and for the gift of a new day we bless Thee. May the strength thus acquired be cheerfully dedicated to the service of Thy Kingdom. As each morning dawns may it witness a new desire in our hearts to grow in faith and to increase in knowledge, to become more like our Master in spirit and in purpose, in self-denial and in true charity. We pray for

PRAYING AS A PASTOR

PRAYERS OF WORSHIP AND DEDICATION

those in the valley who are fighting a fierce battle, and whose life has been one of toil, and struggle, and strain. May they lift their eyes unto the hills, and thus reinforce their drooping energies by Thy grace and strength, and become conscious of a new power, a new courage and a new hope in Jesus Christ. Show us the true ministry of life, that by entering into the troubles of others our own will disappear, that by sharing the burdens of the heavy-laden our own will vanish, that by relieving the poor our riches will increase, through Jesus Christ, our Lord. Amen.

O Thou, in whom we live and have our being! Whose we are, and whom we delight to serve, suffer us to come before Thee with our morning prayer, and to present our bodies a living sacrifice which is our reasonable service. We thank Thee for the pioneers of progress, for devoted saints, for all brave and heroic champions of the faith, who have ever been in ad-

Prayers of Worship and Dedication

vance of their fellows in thought and in action. We bless Thee for their cheerful obedience and for their wholehearted devotion to the work assigned them to do. We see in them Thy best gifts to the world, and in their message Thy love to men. Heavenly Father, help us to feel that we too have a niche to fill and a task to perform; and though that position be far removed from the pathfinder, the crusader, the leader of armies, yet it is possible for us to cheer those who are marching, to succor those who are fighting, to nurse those who have fallen, and to care for those who are dying. Show us that there is room for sacrifice in the rear of the battle, at the prison gate, in the home of affliction, in the chamber of death. Thus with clean and tender hands, with glad and cheerful hearts, may we serve Thee and our fellow man. In Jesus' Name. Amen.

PRAYING AS A
PASTOR

Prayers of Worship and Dedication

O Thou, who are infinite and perfect, our all-seeing, all-knowing and all-loving Father, we come to Thee. Grant us a wider and truer conception of Thyself, and of Thy gracious purpose regarding our sojourn here. Help us to realize, more than we do, that this beautiful world in which we live is Thine, and everything in it, and that we are not our own. We thank Thee for such an inheritance, and for the numerous things that point to one richer, better and more enduring. May we regard this world as our present home, and our life as a sacred trust from Thee. Help us to scatter those seeds that will bear fruit and yield a glorious harvest. May we ever realize that as we sow so shall we reap; as we live here, so we shall live in the future. Give us the strength and the courage to live the immortal life every day — the life of faith and prayer — the life of sunshine and hope — the life that grows brighter and clearer until the perfect day. In the meantime may we make our present inheritance more glo-

Prayers of Worship and Dedication

rious and attractive to others by pointing them to the Saviour of the world as their Friend and Redeemer. May we take every advantage of getting good and of doing good as the days come and go, and in all our efforts may we be prompted and assisted by the Holy Spirit. This we ask in the Name of Christ. Amen.

Out of the depths have we cried unto Thee, O Lord, as we have thought of the magnitude of our sin. If Thou shouldest mark iniquity who could stand? But there is forgiveness with Thee that Thou mayest be feared. Suffer us then to lay at Thy feet the vows we have not kept, the obligations we have failed to meet, and the many transgressions of which we have been guilty. Our hasty words and bitter feelings, our languid wills and cold affections, our wasted moments and selfish ambitions all rise before us, and we find no answer in our heart to the tremendous charge. Our only hope is in the Cross, for the greatness

Prayers of Worship and Dedication

of Thy mercy is the measure of our guilt. May that large and tender word of cheer and comfort uttered on earth by the sinner's Friend be renewed from heaven to us here and now — your sins are forgiven; go in peace. Thus may we enter upon a new chapter in our life, conscious that the past has been forgiven and blotted out. To this end hallow all our inclinations, and purify all our aspirations, and give us a grander conception of the Christian life, and establish our work, seeing we ask all in the Name of our Saviour and divine Lord. Amen.

O Lamb of God, suffer us to gather at the foot of the Cross, there to acknowledge our guilt, there to confess our shortcomings and transgressions, and there to receive from Thine own gracious hand the blessing of absolution. Never can we be sufficiently grateful to Thee for this sacred spot which offers to the truly penitent the gift

Prayers of Worship and Dedication

of solace and rest, the favor of pardon and peace. When we think of our weakness and foolishness in quest of worldly pleasure and gain; when we recall our proneness to evil, and our indifference to the greatest blessing of life, we know not where to look or what to say. Have mercy upon us, O God, and grant us Thy forgiveness. We praise Thee for Thy grace which is mightier than the law, and wider than our need, and higher than our reach, and infinitely more precious than all the gems of earth. By it Thou dost accomplish wonders. The weak are made strong, the unclean are purified, the defiant are reconciled, while those that are afar off are brought nigh. Send out Thy light and Thy truth this day, most merciful Saviour, and may the saving power of the Cross be seen in many hearts, and lives, and homes, and the praise and glory shall be Thine. Amen.

PRAYING AS A PASTOR

Prayers of Worship and Dedication

O Thou, who art the same yesterday, today, and for ever, be pleased to look down upon us with infinite compassion as we invoke Thy favor upon every member of this congregation, and upon those who are unable to meet with us. Separated as we are physically may we be all the more united spiritually. Though deprived of the pleasure of looking into each other's faces, we can all enjoy the great privilege of looking into Thine. For these and all other compensations we humbly thank Thee, and earnestly pray that they may be a means of grace to all concerned. May all the saints this day, on land and sea, in the church and in the home, have such a view of Thee, and of the divine life, that they will be more grateful than ever for the position they occupy and for the work they are called to do. Give us grace to live a day at a time. We are prone to bring back the troubles of yesterday or wonder how we shall cope with the anxieties of tomorrow, and thus deprive ourselves of much joy

Prayers of Worship and Dedication

and pleasure at the present moment. Show us that fret and worry will ever militate against our highest welfare and deepest peace. Remember us one by one as we bow at the Cross, and confess our sins, and renew our vows of fidelity to Thee and to Thy Son. Amen.

Eternal and Holy Father, in the glorious radiance of Thy dear Son we now stand before Thee, and in His omnipotent Name we now pray unto Thee. For the precious thought that calls us to worship, for the love that has provided a place in which to present it, for the calm of this holy day, and for the rich provisions which Thou hast in store for all thirsting souls and wearied pilgrims, we lift to Thee our grateful praise. Awaken within us a new passion for service, a new yearning for the souls of men, a new perception of truth, and a new ambition to live a higher and holier life. Generate within us those graces

Prayers of Worship and Dedication

of character that will make us unremitting in our fidelity to Thee, and uncompromising with the forces of evil. Give us, we pray Thee, an ever widening and deepening interest in the glorious message which Thou hast called us to accept and proclaim, and an ever increasing joy in all that it contains. Forbid that we should ever neglect its teachings or ignore its warnings or despise its appeals. Hear Thou in Heaven Thy dwelling place this our prayer and graciously absolve us from our sins which we now confess before Thee at the Cross in the Name of Him who died upon it — Jesus Christ our Lord. Amen.

Give us, most merciful Father, the secret of waiting upon Thee. Show us how to approach Thee, and teach us how to speak, and what to ask when we come into Thy holy presence. Graciously lift us as a congregation into the heavenly places where we shall see sights, and hear voices that

Prayers of Worship and Dedication

will bring to us renewed strength and courage for our work, and increased joy and confidence in Thee. We have been living and toiling in the lowlands of the world; our feet are covered with the dust of the road; our lips are parched with the heat of the day; our vision has become blurred by unholy sights; and our robes are soiled by contact with evil. Come, blessed Master, with the towel, the basin, and the water and wash our hands and feet and our whole nature, and we shall be clean. Come and light again our lamp so that we may not only see our own way but help to shed a gleam along the dark road of others. Come and rekindle once more the fire upon the altar of our hearts, and then we shall burn with loyalty and enthusiasm in our service for Thee and for our fellow men, and to Thee we will ascribe all the praise and the glory through the atoning work of Thy Son our Saviour. Amen.

SENTENCE PRAYERS

Our Heavenly Father, give us pure hearts that we may have a clearer vision of Thyself and Thy will concerning us.

O Christ, help us to let our light shine that others seeing the good work may glorify Thee.

O God, help us to bear Thy Cross after Thee, for we may by Thy grace.

O Father, help us to walk in the light of Thy presence and have fellowship with Thee.

O Christ, let the light of Thy presence shine through us to influence others to follow Thee.

May the God of all truth and mercy dwell richly in our hearts.

SENTENCE PRAYERS

O Lord, keep us in perfect peace, for we have stayed our mind on Thee.

O God, restore unto us the joy of Thy salvation.

Dear God, our great Shepherd, who not only restores but leads, all through the journey of life, those who trust Him — "Lead us gently home, Father."

I come to Thee, O Christ, praying to know the way to more complete discipleship. In Thy Name.

Dear God, teach me to pray, trusting fully Thy infinite love and Thy unfailing Providence.

Our Heavenly Father, we thank Thee for the privilege of prayer: may we wait patiently before Thee with humble hearts.

Help us, O God, in these distressing days to trust in Thee, with the blessed assurance that Thou doest all things well.

SENTENCE PRAYERS

Dear Father, we are thankful for Thy forgiveness of our sins. Give us strength that we may "go and sin no more."

O God, may the wings of the morning bear us away from darkness and fear and bring to us light and blessed hope.

Protect us by Thy might, great God our King.

O God, help us to redirect our lives toward the great ends of service and kindness and spiritual well-being.

O blessed Christ, we know that in this world we shall have tribulation; but we are of good cheer for Thou hast overcome the world.

O God, help us to put on the whole armor of God, so that we may be able to stand.

O Lord, give us open minds to see ourselves as Thou seest us. We are weak but Thou art strong.

SENTENCE PRAYERS

We thank Thee, O Father, for the power of Thy love, which lifts us and saves us from our sins.

O Lord, we commit our way unto Thee; we know that Thou wilt lead us in the path of righteousness.

"Create in me a clean heart, O God, and renew a right spirit within me."
O Lord, we claim Thy promise that no evil shall befall us and that no plague shall come to our homes.

O Lord, we have sown in tears, but Thou hast promised that we shall reap in joy.

Our Father, we wait upon Thee to strengthen our hearts, for Thou art our refuge and strength, a very present help in trouble.

O Lord, we are troubled on every side, yet not distressed; we are perplexed but not in despair, for in Thee we have strength and salvation.

SENTENCE PRAYERS

O Lord, help us to know that they that are for us are more than all that can come against us.

Help me, O Lord, to possess courage and faith to bear the cross. In Thy Name.

O Father, who commanded the light to shine out of darkness, may it shine in our hearts to give the light of the knowledge of the glory of God in the face of Jesus Christ.

Our Father, give us Thine own spirit of sympathy and love and free us from unkind criticism.

O Lord, sanctify us through the truth; Thy Word is truth.

O Lord, make us to lie down in the green pastures of Thy love, and lead us beside the still waters of Thy grace.

SENTENCE PRAYERS

Our Father, we are commanded to "Rejoice in the Lord alway." May we find real joy in being Christians.

O God, our Father, we thank Thee that Thou art a refuge for us. We have the assurance that Thou wilt ever hear and answer our prayers, through Jesus Christ our Lord.

Help us to go forward today, claiming Thy promise, "I will never leave Thee, nor forsake Thee."

O Lord, God, we thank Thee "that all things work together for good to them that love God." Our lives are not controlled by winds of chance and tides of luck.

Let the words of my mouth and the meditation of my heart be acceptable in Thy sight, O Lord, my strength and my redeemer.